First paperback edition 1997

A CIP catalogue record for this book is available
from the British Library.
ISBN 0-7136-4774-4

First published 1989 in hardback by A & C Black (Publishers) Ltd, 35 Bedford Row, London WC1R 4JH
© 1989, 1997 A & C Black (Publishers) Ltd

Photographs © 1989, 1997 Fiona Pragoff

Acknowledgements
Illustrations by Alex Ayliffe
Science consultant Dr Bryson Gore

The photographer, authors and publishers would like
to thank the following people whose help and
co-operation made this book possible:
Charlene, Abbe, Simon, Ali and their parents.
The staff and pupils at St George's School.

Typeset by Spectrum Typesetting, London
Printed in Singapore by Tien Wah Press (Pte.) Ltd

ROTHERHAM LIBRARY & INFORMATION SERVICES

This book must be returned by the date specified at the time
of issue as the Date Due for Return.
The loan may be extended (personally, by post or telephone)
for a further period, if the book is not required by another
reader, by quoting the above number.

LM1(C)

My Balloon

Kay Davies and Wendy Oldfield
Photographs by Fiona Pragoff

A & C Black · London

Look at all these balloons. How many can you see? What colours and shapes are they?

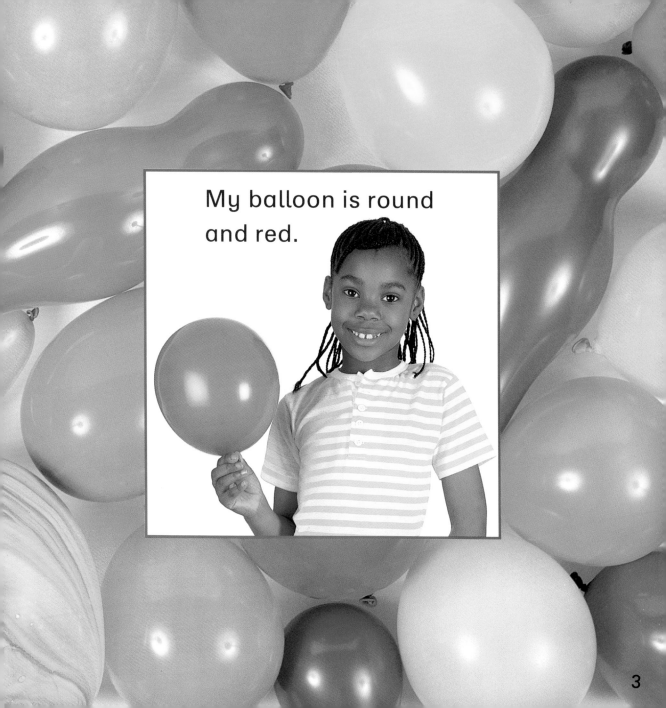

My balloon is round and red.

When I blow air into my balloon,
it stretches and gets bigger.

If I let the air escape,
it makes a hissing noise.

What will happen if I let go?

When I let go of
my balloon, it flies
like a rocket.

6

It makes a funny noise too!

7

I've drawn a face on my balloon.

8

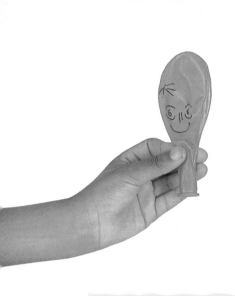

As I blow up my balloon, can you see how the face changes?

To stop the air escaping, Simon is tying string round the neck of my balloon.

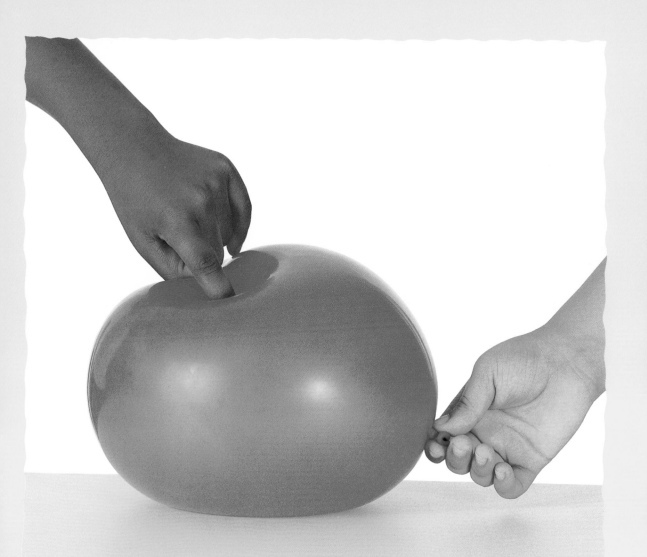

My balloon feels tight and squashy.

If I rub my balloon on my shirt,
it squeaks.

Now I can stick my balloon to the wall.

It's magic!

13

My balloon is very light.
I can pat it up into the air.

Helen is bouncing her balloon
on the table.

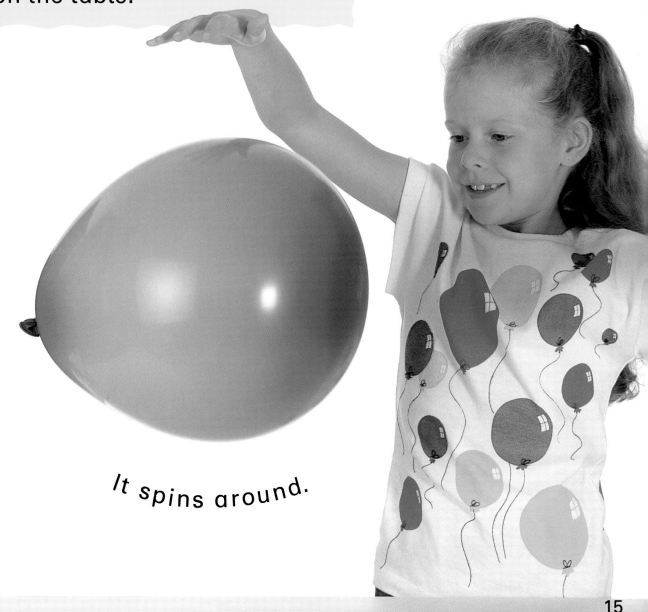

It spins around.

My balloon floats
on water.

Simon can't push his balloon under the water.
If he lets go, what will happen?

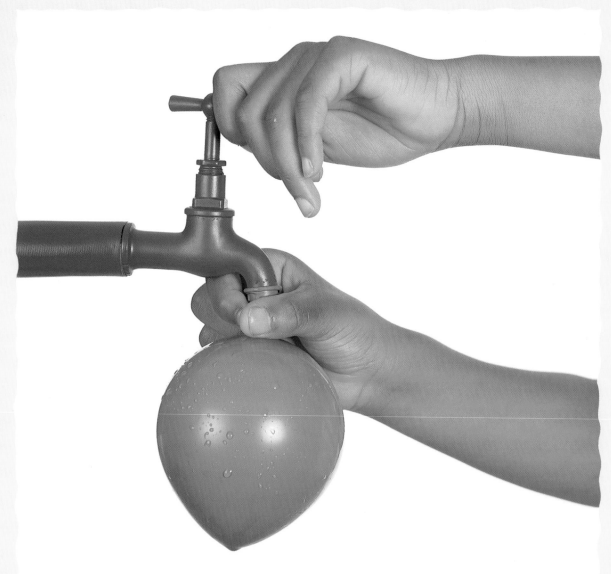

I'm filling my other balloon with water.

It feels much heavier than my red one.

Helen has burst my
red balloon.

Bang!

20

Now it looks small
and wrinkled.

We've got some new balloons which are filled with a special gas.

The gas is very light. It makes the balloons float above our heads.

More things to do

1. Stretchy things
How many other stretchy things can you find? What are they made of? If you stretch them and then let go, do they go back to their original size and shape?

2. Looking through balloons
What can you see through a balloon? How does it change the colour of things? Can you see yourself in a balloon?

3. Balloons and sound
Let the air out of the open neck of a balloon and see how many different sounds you can make. Can you make the sounds higher or lower? Sounds make the air shake to and fro very fast. Hold a balloon and try humming very close to it. Can you feel the balloon shaking as it picks up the shaking movements of the air? What happens if you hold a balloon near to a radio or a television set?

4. Hot-air balloons
Hang a balloon over a radiator. The warm air rising from the radiator will make the balloon bob up and down. See if you can find out about hot-air balloons. What makes them rise up into the sky? How does the pilot control the movements of the balloon and bring it down to land?

5. Ice balloons
Make an ice balloon. Fill a balloon with water and tie the end. Put the balloon inside a plastic bag and leave it in a freezer for a few days. What does the ice balloon feel like? Does it float on water? What happens if you put salt on the ice balloon? Does an ice balloon bounce? How long does an ice balloon take to melt?

Find the page

This list shows you where to find some of the ideas in this book.

Notes for parents and teachers

As you share this book with young children, these notes will help you to explain the scientific concepts behind the different activities.

Pages 2, 3 Colours and shapes
Balloons can be sorted into different groups according to their colour or shape. Before a balloon is blown up, see if the children can guess what it will look like.

Pages 4, 5, 6, 7, 9 Blowing up balloons
A balloon is made of rubber, which is an elastic substance. When you blow up a balloon, it stretches easily, but when you let out the air, it almost goes back to its original size and shape.

Pages 5, 6, 7 Noisy balloons
When air is released through the neck of a balloon, it makes the rubber vibrate, which causes a sound. As the air escapes, it pushes the balloon forwards. A jet engine pushes an aeroplane forwards in a similar way.

Pages 8, 9 Drawing on balloons
As a balloon stretches, any pictures or words become bigger and paler. The shape of the pictures or words is distorted by the curved shape of the balloon.

Pages 10, 11 Trapping the air
It is difficult to compress the air inside a balloon into a smaller space. So, if you press on the surface of a balloon, you force the air into a different shape.

Tiny amounts of air gradually leak out through the surface of a balloon. If a balloon is left for some time, it will eventually go down.

Pages 12, 13 Sticking balloons to the wall
By rubbing a balloon against something, you give it an electrostatic charge, which makes it stick to the wall until the charge leaks away.

Pages 14, 15 Bouncing balloons
A balloon full of air weighs slightly more than the surrounding atmosphere. Although it can be pushed up into the air, it soon sinks back to the ground again under the force of gravity. It comes down quite slowly because of resistance from the air. A balloon bounces rather like a rubber ball.

Pages 16, 17 Floating balloons on water
A balloon is very light for its size. It floats on water because it weighs less than the amount of water it pushes out of the way (displaces).

Pages 18, 19 Light and heavy balloons
Water is much heavier for its size than air – it is more dense. A balloon filled with water is much heavier than one filled with air. (Density is the weight of an object divided by its volume.)

Pages 20, 21 Bursting balloons
There is a limit to the extent to which rubber can be stretched. If a balloon is stretched too much, it bursts. The loud explosion is the sound of the air that was trapped inside rapidly expanding as it is released.

Pages 22, 23 Floating up in the air
If balloons are filled with helium gas, they will float in air because helium is less dense than air.